The Watergate Scandal

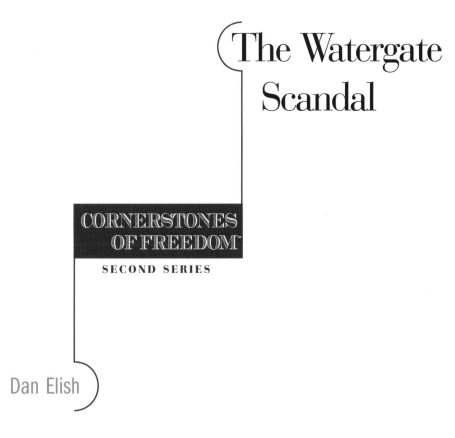

CORNERSTONES OF FREEDOM™

SECOND SERIES

Dan Elish

Children's Press®
A Division of Scholastic Inc.
New York • Toronto • London • Auckland • Sydney
Mexico City • New Delhi • Hong Kong
Danbury, Connecticut

Photographs © 2004: AP/Wide World Photos: 33 (National Archives),
44 top left (stf), 5, 6, 9, 14, 16, 21, 34, 44 bottom, 45 bottom right; Brown
Brothers: 11; Corbis Images: 8, 10, 12, 13, 23, 24 right, 25, 30, 32, 44 top
right, 45 top (Bettmann), 41 (Gennady Galperin/Reuters NewMedia Inc.),
20, 28 (Wally McNamee), 31; Getty Images: 40 (Frank Fisher/Liaison),
4 (Kean Collection); Hulton|Archive/Getty Images: 17 top, 18, 19, 37, 38,
45 bottom left; PictureHistory.com: cover top, 35; Superstock, Inc.: 3;
Time Life Pictures/Getty Images: 17 bottom left, 27 (Gjon Mili), 29 (Steve
Northup), 39 (Bill Pierce), 26; Woodfin Camp & Associates: 17 bottom
right (Robert McElroy), 15 (Jason Laure), 24 left (Susan McElhinney),
cover bottom (Wally McNamee).

Library of Congress Cataloging-in-Publication Data
Elish, Dan.
  The Watergate Scandal / Dan Elish.
    p. cm. — (Cornerstones of freedom. Second series)
  Summary: Detail the events of the scandal called Watergate, including
the major players, how the facts were uncovered, and the way in which
the events ultimately reaffirmed basic principles of the Constitution.
  Includes bibliographical references (p.) and index.
    ISBN 0-516-24239-3
    1. Watergate Affair, 1972-1974—Juvenile literature. [1. Watergate
Affair, 1972–1974. 2. Nixon, Richard M. (Richard Milhous), 1913– 3.
United States—Politics and government—1969–1974.] I. Title. II. Series.
E860.E44 2004
973.924—dc22

                                                2003022794

1 2 3 4 5 6 7 8 9 10 R 13 12 11 10 09 08 07 06 05 04

IT WAS AUGUST 8, 1974. Richard Milhous Nixon, the thirty-seventh president of the United States, had come to the most painful decision of his career. He sat in the Oval Office for the last time and addressed the American people.

"This is the thirty-seventh time I have spoken to you from this office," he began, "where so many decisions have been made that shaped the history of this nation." But this would not be a speech about America's future. Instead Nixon announced that he was resigning, or giving up, the presidency.

Nixon's popularity would prove to be short-lived.

It was a stunning turn of events. Less than two years earlier, President Nixon had been reelected by one of the largest landslides in American history. But on June 17, 1972, police had caught five burglars planting electronic listening devices in the Democratic National Committee headquarters at the Watergate Hotel in Washington, D.C. It was later discovered that Nixon and many of his aides knew about the break-in and had broken the law. Now, a day or two away from being impeached—charged with a crime by Congress—Nixon felt that he had no choice but to quit.

The Watergate scandal caused many Americans to lose faith in their elected leaders. At the same time, Watergate proved that no American is above the law, not even the president.

NIXON'S EARLY CAREER

Richard Milhous Nixon was born on January 19, 1913, in Yorba Linda, a small town in the California desert. When Richard was five, his father moved the family to nearby Whittier and opened a grocery store. Richard often worked in the store when he was growing up.

At Whittier College, Nixon was a member of the second string football team. But he was not as successful in sports as he was in academics. He was known as "the most spirited bench warmer on the team."

But he also found time to study and was an excellent student. At Whittier College he became president of the student body and was on the **debate team**. After getting his law degree at Duke University, Richard Nixon set up a law practice in Whittier.

In December 1941, the United States was attacked

Taken in 1944, this photograph shows Nixon as a
lieutenant commander in
the U.S. Navy.

by Japan at Pearl Harbor, Hawaii, and the country was thrust into World War II. Like most other young men of his era, Nixon joined the armed forces. After serving in the navy, Nixon returned home to Whittier. In 1946, a Republican organization was looking for a "new face" to run for the United States House of Representatives. Impressed with his intelligence, debating skills, and law degree, the group approached young Richard Nixon.

At the time Richard Nixon was getting into politics, the United States and the Soviet Union had emerged as the two most powerful countries in the world. The Soviet Union was based on a system of government called communism, in which a country's wealth was supposed to be shared equally with every citizen. Soviet leader Joseph Stalin, however, was an absolute **dictator** who ruled through fear. He was known to kill his political opponents. Many Americans were scared that communists would enter the United States and take away their basic rights.

In 1946, Nixon ran for Congress against Jerry Voorhis. Voorhis was a well-respected member of the House of Representatives. He had recently been voted the hardest-working man in Congress. But Nixon wasn't scared. In a series of debates, Nixon accused Voorhis of not fighting hard enough against communism. Nixon went on to win the election.

Once he was in Congress, Nixon joined the House Committee on Un-American Activities. Committee members wanted to remove communists from the American government. In a very **controversial** case, Nixon accused

DIRTY TRICKS

During the 1950 campaign for Senate, Helen Gahagan Douglas called Nixon "Tricky Dick." She claimed that he used political "dirty tricks" to help him win. For instance, the Nixon campaign made phony postcards from a well-known communist group expressing support for Douglas.

a well-connected government official named Alger Hiss of being a communist. Nixon played a key role in the investigation, and Hiss was later convicted and went to jail. Now a well-known politician, Nixon ran for the Senate in 1950. Again Nixon stirred up fears of the Soviet Union to help him win. He accused his opponent, Helen Gahagan Douglas, of being in favor of communism.

Nixon's work on the House Committee on Un-American Activities helped to make him a well-known politician. This photograph shows Nixon and other committee members at work in 1948.

THE 'CHECKERS' SPEECH

In 1952, Dwight D. Eisenhower received the Republican nomination for president. The Republican Party wanted someone young who had government experience to run as Eisenhower's vice president. Impressed with Nixon's intelligence and willingness to fight against communism, Eisenhower chose Nixon.

During the campaign, word leaked that Nixon had collected illegal contributions from wealthy businessmen. Nixon said that his votes in the Senate were never influenced, or swayed, by the people who had given him money. Still, many people thought he should quit the race.

This Nixon family portrait was taken in 1952. The family's Cocker Spaniel, Checkers, is on Nixon's lap.

On September 23, 1952, Nixon went on television to declare his innocence. He claimed that all of the money he received had been used to fight communism. At the speech's end, Nixon mentioned that he had kept only one gift—a dog—for his family. Nixon said that his daughter, Trisha, "named it Checkers . . . and I just want to say this, right now, that regardless of what they say about it, we're gonna keep it." Nixon won back the support of much of the country as a result of this speech.

TOUGH LOSSES

Richard Nixon served as vice president under Dwight Eisenhower for eight years. In 1960, Nixon ran for president. That fall, Nixon and his opponent, John F. Kennedy, took part in the first televised presidential debate in American history. Kennedy was a Democratic senator from Massachusetts. Many listeners who heard the debates on radio thought Nixon did a better job. Americans who watched the debates on television thought the handsome Kennedy looked more presidential. That year Nixon lost one of the closest elections in history. Then, in 1962, Nixon ran for

Nixon and Kennedy participated in the first televised presidential debate in U.S. history in 1960.

governor of California and lost again. He later announced to the press, "You won't have Nixon to kick around anymore." It seemed as if Richard Nixon was saying goodbye to public life.

THE NEW NIXON

During the next six years Richard Nixon traveled the country giving speeches for Republican candidates. In 1968, he set his eyes on the White House again. His timing

After losing the 1960 presidential election to John F. Kennedy (left), Nixon would not run for president again until 1968.

Race riots, like this one in Washington, D.C. in April 1968, caused chaos around the country.

was perfect. The 1960s were a **turbulent** time in American history. Led by Dr. Martin Luther King Jr., African Americans began to call for new laws to guarantee their civil rights. College students and so-called hippies took to the streets protesting an unpopular war in Vietnam. Meanwhile, some people didn't like the changes sweeping through America. They were unhappy with new civil rights laws. They also felt angry about various social programs that had been created to help the poor. In 1968, the **assassinations** of Martin Luther King Jr. and U.S. senator Robert Kennedy led to race riots in many American cities.

Nixon's campaign strategy helped him to win the 1968 presidential election. He is shown here in Philadelphia, two months before the election.

VIETNAM

The Vietnam War began in an effort to stop the southern part of Vietnam from being taken over by communists. By the time the war ended in 1975, 58,000 Americans had been killed. Vietnam was the most unpopular war in American history, sparking many antiwar protests.

Now, Nixon promoted himself as someone who could bring the different factions, or groups, of the country together. He said that he wanted "peace with honor" in Vietnam and "law and order" throughout the nation. His strategy worked, but just barely. Nixon defeated his Democratic opponent, Hubert Humphrey, by only a small number of votes.

14

THE PENTAGON PAPERS

Richard Nixon's first term in the White House was marked by some notable achievements. He started the Environmental Protection Agency, a group whose mission was to protect the environment. He expanded the national parks system and oversaw the first Earth Day in 1970.

In foreign affairs, Nixon's early record was mixed. Though he had promised to bring "peace with honor" to Vietnam, Nixon ordered secret bombing runs on nearby Cambodia. When word of what Nixon had done leaked to the press, antiwar protests swept the nation. In June 1971, the antiwar movement gathered even more steam.

Richard Nixon was praised for his work on behalf of the environment. He oversaw the first Earth Day in 1970, when demonstrations like this one took place across the country.

Daniel Ellsberg speaks to reporters in Los Angeles about the Pentagon Papers case.

The *New York Times* began printing a series of secret reports and memos about the United States' bungling of the Vietnam War. This study was known as the Pentagon Papers. One of the men who helped put together this study was Daniel Ellsberg. Ellsberg leaked the reports to the press. He wanted to inform the public about the many lies the United States government had told about the Vietnam War.

The Pentagon Papers' main targets were John Kennedy and Lyndon Johnson, the two previous presidents. But Nixon grew concerned about leaks within his own administration. He tried to bully the *New York Times* into stopping the publication of the Pentagon Papers. When that didn't work he turned to the courts. On June 30, 1971, the Supreme Court ruled that American newspapers had the right to print the papers.

Shortly after, Nixon organized a White House team to spy on Ellsberg. A former Central Intelligence Agency (CIA) operative named E. Howard Hunt Jr. and a former agent with the Federal Bureau of Investigations (FBI), G. Gordon Liddy, were hired to lead the unit. They were jokingly called the plumbers because their job was to stop leaks, but what they were up to wasn't funny. The plumbers' first job was to break into the office of Ellsberg's **psychiatrist**. They were looking for any material that might make Ellsberg look bad. Indeed, Nixon's new team was ready to do whatever it took to protect the president.

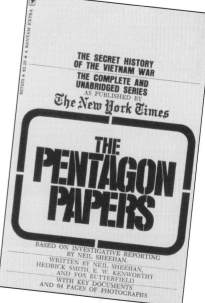

The publication of the Pentagon Papers sparked an important legal battle about freedom of the press.

E. Howard Hunt Jr. (left) and G. Gordon Liddy (right) were hired by President Nixon to stop information "leaks" to the press.

THE FIRST AMENDMENT

The First Amendment to the United States Constitution states that "Congress must not interfere with freedom of religion, speech or press, assembly, and petition." This is the reason why the Supreme Court ruled that the *New York Times* had the right to continue publishing the Pentagon Papers.

The Watergate apartment complex will always be known as the site of the infamous 1972 break-in.

THE BREAK-IN

"I decided that we must begin immediately keeping track of everything the leading Democrats did," Nixon wrote later in

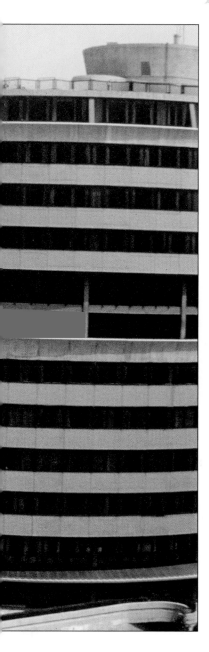

his life. "Information would be our first line of defense." In addition, Nixon's advisers set up an organization called the Committee to Reelect the President (CREEP) that was used to create a "slush" fund of money. This money would be used to play "dirty tricks" on Democrats. Some dirty tricks were silly, such as ordering three hundred dollars' worth of pizza for a Democratic fundraiser and leaving Democrats to pay the bill. Others were more harmful.

Meanwhile, Nixon's plumbers unit was busy plugging up "leaks." But no one outside of a small group of men close to the White House knew about it—until the plumbers got caught.

On June 17, 1972, three policemen responded to a call at 1:52 A.M. about a break-in at the Watergate apartment building in downtown Washington. Frank Wills, the security guard on duty, showed the police door latches in the parking garage that had been covered with tape. The police then followed clues up to the sixth floor. There, at the headquarters of the

Watergate burglars James McCord and Eugenio Martinez are escorted from the courthouse.

Democratic National Committee, they found files strewn across the floor. Then all of a sudden, "five middle-aged guys stood up," Officer John Barrett said later, "wearing suits and ties and surgical gloves."

This was the second time the burglars had broken into the Watergate. Earlier in the month, they had broken in and placed electronic bugs, or illegal listening devices, on the telephones. This allowed Nixon's advisers to hear private conversations. When the bugs weren't working properly, the burglars had been forced to make a return trip. This time they were caught red-handed. Three of the five—Bernard Barker, Virgilio Gonzales, and Eugenio Martinez—were of Cuban descent. They had been hired by the Nixon campaign to help with the burglary. A fourth, Frank Sturgis, was also called one of "the Cubans," even though he was American. The fifth man was James W. McCord, a former FBI agent and the security director of CREEP. All five men carried a series of unmarked one-hundred-dollar bills. Later G. Gordon Liddy and E. Howard Hunt Jr. were connected to the crime and also arrested. The White House press secretary, Ron Ziegler, called the break-in "a third-rate burglary attempt."

WOODWARD AND BERNSTEIN

Much of the credit for bringing these crimes out into the open belongs to two young reporters from the *Washington Post* named Bob Woodward and Carl Bernstein. The two men could not have been more different. Twenty-nine-year-old

As a result of their Watergate investigation, Carl Bernstein and Bob Woodward became the most famous **journalists** of the twentieth century.

NEW JOURNALISM

Woodward and Bernstein's book, *All the President's Men*, tells how they gathered the information that uncovered the Watergate scandal. This famous book is now used as a handbook for young journalists. It demonstrates what Ben Bradlee, the editor-in-chief at the *Post*, called Woodward and Bernstein's most important contribution to American journalism: their persistence. As Bradlee put it, "They had no qualms about calling a source back and back and back."

Woodward was a graduate of Yale University. He had been at the paper for only nine months. Twenty-eight-year-old Bernstein was a high-school dropout who had started at the *Post* as a copy boy at age sixteen. Together they would uncover a series of crimes that ended Richard Nixon's presidency.

The day after the break-in, Woodward went to court to watch the five men who had been captured stand before the judge. When James McCord admitted that he used to work for the CIA, America's secret spy agency, Woodward sensed that this could be an important story.

Even so, it took a while for the Watergate story to catch fire with the public. Though the *Washington Post* and the FBI were able to trace James McCord directly to CREEP, members of the Nixon administration said that the burglars had acted on their own and not at the direction of the president. On June 22, President Nixon stated during a press conference that "this kind of activity . . . has no place whatever in our electoral process." Most Americans believed the White House was not involved.

Still, Woodward and Bernstein kept digging for clues. They wanted to find out where the burglars' money came from and who controlled it. On August 1, they reported that a cashier's check for $25,000 that had been meant for President Nixon's reelection campaign had found its way into the bank account of one of the men arrested in the break-in. Later, they finally convinced Hugh Sloan, the treasurer of CREEP, to talk. Sloan admitted that a few senior people at the White House knew about the dirty activities of the plumbers unit.

Woodward and Bernstein
followed every lead in an
effort to uncover the
truth about the
Watergate scandal.

On September 29, 1972, the *Post* published a shocking front-page article. It stated that John Mitchell, while serving as the United States attorney general, controlled a

U.S. Attorney General John V. Mitchell was thought to be linked to the Watergate break-in.

fund that was used to gather information about Democrats. The night before the story was released, Carl Bernstein called Mitchell to give him a chance to comment on the article. Mitchell exploded, saying, "That's the most sickening thing I ever heard!"

Many people felt that the *Washington Post* was being unfair to Nixon and his men. By the time of the presidential election a little more than a month later, only half of the country had even heard of Watergate. Nixon won by a landslide.

President Nixon and Vice President Spiro Agnew wave to supporters after winning the 1972 election.

DEEP THROAT

Many reporters rely on "anonymous sources," or people who supply information but who don't want to be named in the newspaper. Bob Woodward's source had access to information from the White House, the FBI, and CREEP. Jokingly named Deep Throat by an editor at the *Washington Post*, this source secretly met with Woodward during the Watergate investigation to offer advice. Woodward has kept Deep Throat's identity secret to this day.

Four members of the "Watergate Seven," Virgilio Gonzales, Bernard Barker, Frank Sturgis, and Eugenio Martinez, walk to the courthouse in Washington, D.C. Attorney Henry Rothblatt is shown front center.

TRIAL OF THE WATERGATE SEVEN

On January 8, 1973, the five burglars plus the masterminds, E. Howard Hunt and G. Gordon Liddy, went on trial in Washington, D.C. The judge was John Sirica, a crusty sixty-nine-year-old who was a year away from retirement. Barker, Gonzales, Martinez, and Sturgis pleaded guilty, but Judge Sirica showed that he would stop at nothing to reach the truth. "Don't pull any punches," he told them. "You give me straight answers." But despite repeated questioning, the burglars did not say that any senior aides in the White House were involved. They insisted that the entire operation was planned by Liddy and Hunt. When Sirica asked them who supplied the money, the burglars said that they didn't know. Sirica snapped, "Well, I'm sorry, but I don't believe you." On January 30, 1973, a jury found Liddy and McCord guilty of **conspiracy**, burglary, and **wiretapping**.

25

On March 19 one of the Watergate Seven finally decided to tell the truth. Just before his sentencing, James McCord handed Judge Sirica a letter. McCord wrote that he and the other defendants had lied at the urging of John Mitchell and John Dean, Nixon's lawyer. McCord also wrote that John Mitchell had approved the Watergate wiretapping. All the defendants had been given money in return for their silence.

McCord's statement blew the case wide open. On March 21, John Dean told the president, "We have a cancer within—close to the presidency—that's growing . . ." Instead of telling the truth, Nixon decided to cover up his involvement even more. It was later discovered that Nixon told some

Bob Haldeman (left) and John Erlichman (center, seated) both resigned at Nixon's request.

chief advisers that a million dollars could be raised to buy the silence of key witnesses. Nixon grew more and more nervous that he would be directly accused of covering up the Watergate crimes. He decided to let two of his chief advisers take the blame. On April 30, Nixon made an announcement on television. He said that he had accepted the resignations of John Erlichman and Robert Haldeman, two top aides who had been **implicated** in the Watergate cover-up. He also fired John Dean. Richard Nixon was feeling the heat.

THE SENATE WATERGATE COMMITTEE

By this time, the members of the United States Senate were concerned about Watergate. On February 7, 1973, they voted to set up a committee to investigate the break-in. The committee's chairman was Senator Sam Ervin. The nation watched on television as witness after witness **testified** that various members of the White House had been involved in Nixon's plumbers unit or in the Watergate cover-up.

Even though important officials in Nixon's administration were accused, no one said that Nixon himself had been involved in the crimes. This changed on June 25, when John Dean took the stand. Dean stated that Nixon himself had known

Senator Sam Ervin was a lawyer from North Carolina who was known to be fair.

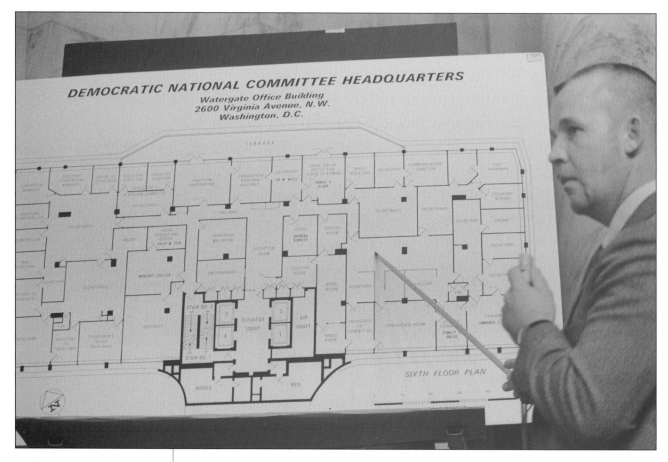

A police investigator explains the details of the break-in during the Watergate hearings.

about the Watergate cover-up from the beginning. In later testimony, however, Bob Haldeman and John Erlichman said that Dean was lying. They insisted that Nixon didn't know anything about the break-in.

Then, former deputy assistant to the president, Alexander Butterfield, testified before the committee. On July 16, he was asked if President Nixon had some sort of recording system in the Oval Office of the White House. Butterfield sighed and said, "I was hoping you fellows wouldn't ask me that." Butterfield admitted that Nixon

* * * *

had tapes of every conversation he had had in the Oval Office since 1971. Finally the Watergate Committee had a way to find out once and for all what Richard Nixon knew and when he knew it.

FIGHT FOR THE TAPES

On July 23, Archibald Cox, the special prosecutor in charge of investigating Watergate, and the Senate committee demanded that Nixon hand over the tapes and other White House documents. Two days later Nixon refused.

29

On July 26, the Watergate Committee issued a subpoena. This is a document that commands a person to appear in court or to produce evidence to investigators. The subpoena required Nixon to deliver the tapes.

Nixon claimed that he had executive privilege. He felt that it was the right of the president to keep certain tapes and

documents out of the hands of Congress and the courts. In other words, Nixon argued that only a president could decide what documents and tapes would hurt national security if made public. Again, the issue went to Judge Sirica. Sirica ruled that he wanted to hear the tapes personally. In October another court upheld Sirica's decision, writing: "Though the President is elected by nation-wide ballot and is often said to represent all the people, he . . . is not above the law's commands."

Judge John J. Sirica ordered the White House to produce the tapes. The U.S. Supreme Court upheld his decision.

THE SATURDAY NIGHT MASSACRE

Richard Nixon was stubborn. He continued to refuse turning over the tapes. On October 19, 1973, he proposed a compromise: He would allow Senator John Stennis to listen to some of the tapes and prepare **transcripts** for the rest of the Watergate Committee. What followed became known as the Saturday Night Massacre—not because anyone was killed, but because several senior White House officials lost their jobs. When Cox refused Nixon's compromise, Nixon asked Attorney General Elliot Richardson to fire him. Richardson refused and resigned in protest. Then Nixon asked the deputy attorney general,

A NEW VICE PRESIDENT

Nixon's troubles grew when his vice president, Spiro Agnew, was forced to resign on October 10, 1973, for not paying his taxes. Two days later, Nixon nominated Gerald Ford, a congressman from Michigan, to be his new vice president. Ford was widely respected as a man of great character and honesty. He was sworn in as vice president on December 6, 1973.

This political cartoon pokes fun at the Watergate Scandal. It shows a huge reel of audiotape crashing onto the White House.

Suares '73

Two men unload transcripts of the Nixon tapes.

William Ruckelshaus, to fire Cox. Ruckelshaus also refused and was fired. Finally, the solicitor general, Robert Bork, agreed to fire Cox. "Whether ours shall continue to be a government of laws and not of men," Cox said, "is now for the Congress and ultimately the American people to decide."

As it turned out, the American people were outraged by the dismissals. Under pressure, Nixon agreed to release some of the tapes. But on October 30, White House counsel Fred Buzhardt told Judge Sirica that, although nine tapes had been requested, two of the tapes were "nonexistent" because they had never been made. Most Americans felt the Nixon administration was lying.

Things continued to get worse. On November 21, Buzhardt told Judge Sirica that a gap of eighteen and a half minutes was discovered on one of the tapes. The gap occurred during a June 20, 1972, conversation between Nixon and his chief of staff, Bob Haldeman. The White House claimed that Nixon's personal secretary had accidentally erased five minutes of the tapes. But electronics experts testified to what everyone suspected: The eighteen-and-a-half-minute tape had been purposely erased.

EIGHTEEN AND A HALF MINUTES

When the White House claimed that part of Nixon's tapes had been accidentally erased, many people grew **skeptical**. *The National Review*, a magazine that had supported Nixon in the past, wrote: "Believers in the accidental theory could gather for lunch in a phone booth."

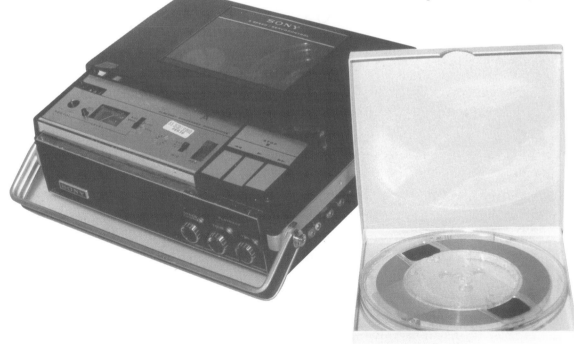

This photograph shows the original Nixon White House tape recorder and one of the tapes. Altogether, the White House recorded about 2,800 hours of conversation.

President Nixon delivers the State of the Union address in January 1974. Gerald Ford is seated behind him.

★ ★ ★ ★

ROAD TO IMPEACHMENT

Things were looking grim for Richard Nixon. In his State of the Union address in January 1974, Nixon promised to cooperate with the Watergate Committee. However, he also added that he would never do "anything that weakens the Office of the President of the United States or impairs the ability of the presidents of the future to make the great decisions." On one hand Nixon was promising to cooperate. On the other he made it clear that he would continue to claim executive privilege as a reason for not releasing the tapes.

By February 1974, the House of Representatives had made a decision. They would allow the House Judiciary Committee to investigate whether there was reason to impeach the president. On April 16, another subpoena was issued. Again Nixon refused, but he did release more edited transcripts of the tapes. Although none of the tapes placed blame on Nixon for the Watergate crimes, the country was horrified by their tone. In the tapes, Nixon cursed frequently. He

In April 1974, Nixon agreed to release more edited transcripts of the tapes relating to the Watergate break-in.

IMPEACHED

When a president is believed to have committed a crime, members of the House of Representatives may bring charges against him or her. This charge is called an impeachment. It is then the right of the Senate to hold a trial and vote on whether to remove the official from office. Only two American presidents, Andrew Johnson (1865–1869) in 1868, and Bill Clinton (1993–2001) in 1998, have been impeached. Both were acquitted (declared innocent) by the Senate and allowed to stay in office.

sounded mean-spirited and too concerned about enemies who would "do us in." "This is war," he said to John Dean in 1972. "They are after us."

The House Judiciary Committee began impeachment hearings on May 9. In June, Nixon desperately tried to turn the country's attention away from Watergate by making a tour of the Middle East and the Soviet Union. He returned to bad news. On July 24, the Supreme Court ruled that Nixon must release all the tapes.

A PRESIDENT RESIGNS

As the evidence against him mounted, President Nixon hoped that enough Republicans in the House of Representatives would vote against any motion to impeach. His hopes were soon dashed. On July 27, the House Judiciary Committee adopted the first article of impeachment. It charged the president with obstructing—or trying to stop—the Watergate investigation.

The president released the final tapes and hoped for a miracle. It did not come. One of the recordings was especially damaging. On June 23, 1972, Nixon had ordered his chief of staff to tell the FBI to call off the investigation into the Watergate break-in. It was the proof that many Americans had been looking for. Richard Nixon had finally been caught red-handed trying to cover up a crime against the Democratic Party.

Within twenty-four hours after the release of the final tapes, every member of the House Judiciary Committee said that Nixon should resign. On August 7, three important Republicans visited the president. Nixon asked how many votes he could count on in the Senate. Senator Barry Goldwater replied, "Ten at most, maybe less." Shortly after that, Nixon made his decision.

At nine o'clock on August 8, President Nixon addressed the nation. He never admitted that he had committed any crimes. He only confessed to showing poor judgment. "I would say only that if some of my judgments

Members of the House Judiciary Committee discuss whether President Nixon should be impeached.

On August 8, 1974, the front page of the *New York Post* announced Nixon's resignation.

were wrong—and some were wrong—they were made in what I believed at the time to be the best interests of the nation."

The following morning, Richard Nixon formally resigned. He then delivered a farewell address to the White House staff. Gerald Ford was sworn in as the thirty-eighth president of the United States while Nixon and his wife, Pat, boarded a helicopter for their home in California.

President Nixon gives one final wave before leaving the White House.

Gerald Ford took the oath of office as the 38th president after Richard Nixon resigned.

THE PARDON

After he left office, Richard Nixon faced criminal charges that might have put him in jail. But on September 8, 1974, President Gerald Ford granted Nixon a "full, free, and absolute" **pardon** for "all offenses against the United States." Ford argued that it was time for the nation to put Watergate behind it. Still, many Americans were outraged. When Ford ran for president two years later in 1976, many Americans voted against him because of the pardon.

LEGACY OF WATERGATE

President Nixon died in 1994. Even though he had resigned in shame, he later managed to become a well-respected expert on foreign affairs. Many of the president's staff who were involved in Watergate served short prison sentences.

Watergate had an enormous effect on the country. Congress passed laws to control how much money a person or a company could give to a candidate. Congress also passed a law that gave the attorney general the right to name a special prosecutor to investigate any member of the government suspected of being involved in illegal activities.

Even so, it is clear that Watergate could easily happen again. In the 1980s, aides of President Ronald Reagan illegally funded a war in Nicaragua by selling weapons in Iran. In 1998, President Bill Clinton was impeached for lying under oath about having a romantic relationship with a young woman in his office. In 2001, Vice President Dick Cheney once again claimed "executive privilege" when he refused to give documents about the administration's energy policy to Congress. And rich donors are still able to influence the political system by giving millions of dollars to their favorite candidates. In the end, it is up to each generation of Americans to demand that their leaders remain honest.

Later in life, Nixon earned praise for his work in foreign affairs. He is shown here with Boris Yeltsin, the president of Russia, in 1992.

Glossary

assassination—murder, often for political reasons

conspiracy—a plan by a group of people to commit an unlawful act

controversial—causing people to react with strong opposing views

debate team—an organization that meets with other teams to present arguments for and against a particular idea

dictator—a person who holds absolute power

implicated—accused of helping to commit a crime

journalist—a writer for newspapers and magazines

pardon—to release someone from the legal penalties of a crime

psychiatrist—a doctor who treats mental disorders

skeptical—doubtful

testified—stated a fact under oath

transcripts—written, word-for-word records of what was said

turbulent—relating to unrest, violence, or a disturbance

wiretapping—illegally planting electronic listening devices in telephones

Timeline: The Watergate

1968 1972   1973

NOVEMBER
Richard M. Nixon is elected president.

JUNE
Five burglars are arrested during a break-in at the Democratic National Committee headquarters in the Watergate Hotel in Washington, D.C.

SEPTEMBER
The *Washington Post* reports that John Mitchell, while attorney general, controlled a secret Republican fund that was used to finance "dirty tricks" against Democrats.

NOVEMBER
Richard M. Nixon is reelected president.

JANUARY
The trial of the "Watergate Seven" begins.

MARCH
James W. McCord writes a letter to Judge John Sirica. It states that he and the other defendants lied at the urging of the White House.

MAY
The Senate Watergate Committee begins its televised hearings.

JUNE
John Dean testifies before the Watergate Committee. He claims that Nixon was involved in the cover-up of the Watergate burglary.

Scandal

1974

JULY
Alexander Butterfield tells the Senate Watergate Committee that President Nixon has taped White House conversations since 1971.

AUGUST
Nixon claims "executive privilege" and refuses to hand over any tapes.

OCTOBER
The "Saturday Night Massacre" takes place. Nixon fires special prosecutor Archibald Cox and accepts the resignations of Attorney General Elliot Richardson and Deputy Attorney General William Ruckelshaus.

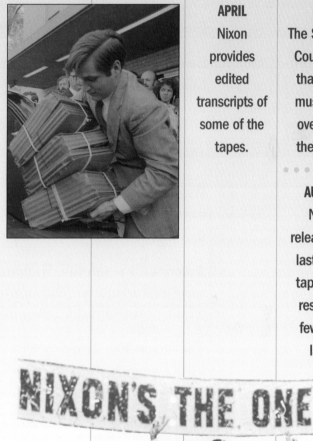

APRIL
Nixon provides edited transcripts of some of the tapes.

JULY
The Supreme Court rules that Nixon must hand over all of the tapes.

AUGUST
Nixon releases the last of the tapes and resigns a few days later.

THE SECRET HISTORY OF THE VIETNAM WAR
THE COMPLETE AND UNABRIDGED SERIES AS PUBLISHED BY
The New York Times

THE PENTAGON PAPERS

BASED ON INVESTIGATIVE REPORTING BY NEIL SHEEHAN.
WRITTEN BY NEIL SHEEHAN, HEDRICK SMITH, E. W. KENWORTHY AND FOX BUTTERFIELD.
WITH KEY DOCUMENTS AND 64 PAGES OF PHOTOGRAPHS

NIXON'S THE ONE

To Find Out More

BOOKS

Cohen, Daniel. *Watergate: Deception in the White House.* Brookfield, CT: Millbrook Press, 1998.

Green, Robert. *Richard M. Nixon.* New York: Compass Point Books, 2003.

ONLINE SITES

Washington Post—Revisiting Watergate
www.washingtonpost.com/wp-srv/national/longterm/watergate/front.htm

American Presidents, Richard M. Nixon
www.americanpresidents.org/presidents/president.asp?PresidentNumber=36

The Nixon Era Times
www.watergate.com

MOVIES

All the President's Men (1976)

Index

Bold numbers indicate illustrations.

About the Author

Dan Elish is the author of numerous books for children, including *The Worldwide Dessert Contest* and *Born Too Short, The Confessions of an Eighth-Grade Basket Case*, which was picked as a 2003 Book for the Teen Age by the New York Public Library. He lives in New York City with his wife and daughter.